Pass Out

Pass Out

80 cocktails to paint the town red

MQP

An Hachette Livre Company
First published in Great Britain in 2003 by
MQ Publications,
a division of Octopus Publishing Group Ltd
2–4 Heron Quays, London E14 4JP
www.octopusbooks.co.uk

Copyright © Octopus Publishing Group Ltd,
2003, 2008

ISBN: 978-184072-509-4

10 9 8 7 6 5 4 3 2

Printed and bound in China

This book contains the opinions and ideas of the
publisher. It is intended to provide helpful and
informative material on the subjects addressed in
this book and is sold with the understanding that
the publisher is not engaged in rendering any
kind of personal professional services in this
book. The publisher disclaims all responsibility
for any liability, loss, or risk, personal or
otherwise, which is incurred as a consequence,
directly or indirectly, of the use and application of
any of the contents of this book.

Weights and Measurements

The recipes in this book are based on the
measurements for one drink. However,
ingredients are given in ratio form to make
it easy to mix a greater number of
cocktails. For one drink, one "part"
corresponds to 1fl oz US or 30ml. You can
use whatever type of measure you like; a
pony holds 1fl oz US, a jigger 1½fl oz US.

Liquid ingredients:

dash	⅙fl oz	2ml
bar spoon	½fl oz	15ml
1 tsp	⅙fl oz	5ml
1 tbsp (3 tsp)	½fl oz	15ml
2 tbsp (pony)	1fl oz	30ml
3 tbsp (jigger)	1½fl oz	45ml
¼ cup	2fl oz	60ml
⅓ cup	2½fl oz	80ml
½ cup	4fl oz	125ml
⅔ cup	5fl oz	160ml
¾ cup	6fl oz	180ml
1 cup	8fl oz	250ml
1 pint US	16fl oz	500ml

Dry ingredients:

	1in	2.5cm
	1oz	25g

Glossary

The following culinary terms will provide
useful guidelines for international readers
to follow.

heavy cream	double cream
light cream	single cream
pitted	stoned
scallion	spring onion
carambola	star fruit

Introduction

Take off that power suit, dust down your cocktail shaker, and invite some friends around—it's Friday night, and that means . . . it's cocktail hour!

Combining the classic with the innovative, the sophisticated with the unashamedly garish, Pass Out is a hip and high-spirited introduction to the intoxicating art of mixology.

Looking for a sleek and sexy love potion to wow your partner? Go straight to The New Romantics for a profusion of sultry aphrodisiacs. Searching for a summer sizzler to temper the heat of the midday sun? Look no further than Club Tropicana. Or perhaps you want something truly hardcore to kick-start a night on the town? Choose from our selection of devilish Super Sharp Shooters!

If you've ever wondered how to create the ultimate Dry Martini, shaken, not stirred, or how to give your Margarita glass the perfect salt rim, this is the book for you. Pass Out contains a wealth of helpful hints and bartender's tips that will aid you in your quest to become a veritable cocktail genius— you'll be pumping your cocktail shaker faster than you can say Tequila Sunrise!

1

The Usual Suspects

Authentic originals

Dry Martini

No other cocktail arouses so much controversy as the Dry Martini. The ratio of gin to vermouth varies wildly. Here is the classic '50s version.

4 parts gin
1 part dry vermouth
Two pitted green olives,
  to garnish

Shake the ingredients vigorously in a cocktail shaker with cracked ice. Strain into a chilled cocktail glass and serve straight up. Garnish with two pitted green olives.

Long Island Iced Tea

This popular cocktail dates back to Prohibition times, so don't be fooled by its innocuous name and pale brown color! A cool, refreshing happy-hour favorite, it is great for sipping on the veranda on a balmy summer evening.

½ part golden rum
½ part gin
½ part vodka
½ part tequila
½ part Cointreau or
  triple sec
½ part sugar syrup (see p. 33)
1 part freshly squeezed
  lime juice
Dash of cola
Wedge of lime, to garnish

Combine all the ingredients, except the cola, in a cocktail shaker with cracked ice. Shake well. Strain into a highball glass half-filled with ice. Top up with a dash of cola and garnish with a wedge of lime.

Dry Martini

Bloody Mary

Bloody Mary

Vodka drinks gained popularity in the '50s. This rich red concoction was, then as now, perfect as a pick-me-up or hangover buster. You can create your own signature recipe with the addition or subtraction of numerous additional ingredients, including horseradish, dill, and jalepeño juice.

1 part vodka
2 parts tomato juice
¼ part freshly squeezed
   lemon juice
1 tsp Worcestershire sauce
2 dashes of Tabasco sauce
1 pinch celery salt
Celery stalk, to garnish

Shake the ingredients gently in a cocktail shaker with cracked ice to keep the tomato juice from separating. Pour into a chilled highball or Collins glass. Garnish with a celery stalk.

Bartender's Tip

Attractive natural stirrers or swizzle sticks can be easily fashioned from a bamboo sprig, a stem of lemon grass, a celery stick, a cinnamon stick, or a length of cucumber.

Applejack

The early American settlers distilled hard cider to make applejack and drank it neat. By the '50s, however, tastes had become a little more refined!

1 part applejack
1 part grapefruit juice
Dash of grenadine
Twist of lemon peel,
  to garnish

Stir or shake the ingredients with cracked ice. Strain into a cocktail glass filled with crushed ice and garnish with a twist of lemon peel.

Whiskey Sour

Sour by name, sour by nature, this traditional gentleman's drink should be served plain and simple in an old-fashioned glass.

2 parts rye whisky
1 part freshly squeezed
  lemon juice
1 tsp sugar
Twist of lemon peel,
  to garnish

Shake the ingredients vigorously in a cocktail shaker with cracked ice, until foamy. Pour into a chilled old-fashioned glass. Garnish with a twist of lemon peel.

Mint Julep

Mint Julep

The first Saturday in May—the running of the Kentucky Derby—is the traditional start of the Mint Julep season. The Derby can take credit for the widespread popularity of this delightfully thirst-quenching drink, but feel free to enjoy one any time, whether you're watching the race or not!

1 tsp sugar
1 tbsp chopped mint leaves
1 tbsp water
1½ parts bourbon
Sprig of fresh mint,
  to garnish

Put the sugar and chopped mint in a mortar and bruise the leaves with a pestle to make a paste. Add the water and continue pounding. Fill a highball glass or a goblet half-full with crushed ice. Add the mint syrup and bourbon. Fill the glass with more crushed ice and tuck the sprig of mint into the ice with a couple of short straws.

Classic Cocktail

Not to be confused with a Classic Champagne Cocktail (see page 22), this is a cool and sophisticated drink that will make you feel one in a million!

1½ parts brandy
½ part curaçao
½ part maraschino
½ part freshly squeezed
  lime juice
½ part sugar syrup (see p. 33)
Maraschino cherries,
  to garnish

Shake the ingredients in a cocktail shaker with cracked ice. Strain into a cocktail glass. Serve straight up and garnish with maraschino cherries.

Rusty Nail

The Drambuie in this cocktail sweetens and softens the Scotch with its subtle heather tones. Refreshingly simple, the Rusty Nail is a great favorite with Scotch-drinkers the world over.

2 parts Scotch
1 part Drambuie
Twist of lemon peel,
  to garnish

Combine the ingredients with ice in a mixing glass and stir with a glass swizzle stick. Strain into an old-fashioned glass filled with ice cubes. Garnish with a long twist of lemon peel.

Sidecar

This zingy little cocktail is a fantastic winter warmer!

3 parts brandy
1 part Cointreau or
  triple sec
1 part freshly squeezed
  lemon juice
Garnish
Twist of lemon peel
Maraschino cherry

Shake the ingredients vigorously in a cocktail shaker with cracked ice. Strain into a chilled cocktail glass and serve straight up with a twist of lemon peel and a maraschino cherry.

Rusty Nail

Bellini

Invented in the '40s at Harry's Bar in Venice, the fragrant peach-flavored Bellini cocktail caught on with Americans in the '50s.

3 parts chilled dry
  champagne
1 part chilled peach juice
Thin slice of peach,
  to garnish

Pour the champagne and peach juice into a chilled champagne saucer glass. Stir lightly with a glass swizzle stick. Garnish with a thin slice of peach.

Old-fashioned

This simple, venerable whisky cocktail has always been a great favorite. Bring it up to date with some wacky accessories and garnishes!

½ tsp sugar
2 dashes of Angostura bitters
1 tsp water
1½ parts rye whisky
Garnish
Slice of orange
Slice of pineapple
Maraschino cherry

Put the sugar in an old-fashioned glass. Add the bitters and water. Muddle to dissolve the sugar. Add the rye whisky and an ice cube and stir with a glass swizzle stick. Garnish with a slice of orange, a slice of pineapple, and a maraschino cherry.

Stinger

Use white crème de menthe for the authentic '50s version of this cocktail.

2 parts brandy
2 parts white crème
  de menthe
1 part freshly squeezed
  lime juice
Twist of lime, to garnish

Combine the ingredients in a cocktail shaker with cracked ice. Shake well and strain into a chilled highball glass. Serve straight up and garnish with a twist of lime.

Classic Champagne Cocktail

The epitome of sophistication, the Classic Champagne Cocktail can be served in one of two different glasses: flute, or saucer-shaped champagne glass.

1 cube of sugar
1 tsp brandy
3 dashes of
  Angostura bitters
Chilled dry champagne
Twist of lemon peel,
  to garnish

Put the cube of sugar into a chilled champagne glass. Sprinkle with the brandy and the Angostura bitters. Pour the champagne into the glass and stir lightly with a glass swizzle stick to mix. Garnish with a twist of lemon peel.

Stinger

Margarita

Margarita

The Margarita's origins, like those of all classic cocktails, are shrouded in legend. Its native home is Mexico. Tales tell of a beautiful woman named Margarita, thwarted love, and a bartender who created a drink in her memory.

Wedge of lime and salt,
   for frosting
2 parts tequila
1 part Cointreau or
   triple sec
½ part freshly squeezed
   lime juice
Wedge of lime, to garnish

Rub a wedge of lime round the rim of a chilled cocktail or margarita glass, then dip into a saucer of fine salt to frost. Shake the ingredients vigorously in a cocktail shaker with cracked ice. Strain into the glass. Serve straight up, garnished with a wedge of lime.

Bartender's Tip

The rim of a cocktail glass may be decorated with salt, sugar, or even chocolate. The salt frosting on the rim of a Margarita glass is achieved by running a wedge of lemon or lime around the rim while holding it upside down to prevent the juice from running down the side of the glass. Next, dip the rim of the glass into a saucer of salt until evenly coated. For sugary frostings, dip the rim of the glass into a little water, or a wet sponge, and then into a saucer of sugar. For added effect, consider using food coloring or vegetable dye to match the color of the frosting to that of the drink.

Sloe Gin Fizz

Combined deliciously with sweet vermouth and club soda, sloe gin liquor becomes sparkling heaven in a glass!

3 parts sloe gin
2 parts sweet vermouth
1 part freshly squeezed
  lemon juice
Club soda

Shake the gin, vermouth, and lemon juice vigorously in a cocktail shaker with cracked ice. Strain into a highball glass. Add ice cubes and fill the glass with club soda.

Tom Collins

Sweet, sugary, and sophisticated, this drink lends its name to the Collins glass, an essential piece of glassware for any serious bartender!

2 parts gin
1 part freshly squeezed
  lemon juice
1 part sugar syrup (see p. 33)
Club soda
Sprig of fresh mint leaves,
  to garnish

Shake the gin, lemon juice, and sugar syrup thoroughly in a cocktail shaker with cracked ice. Strain into a Collins glass. Add ice cubes and fill the glass with club soda. Garnish with a sprig of fresh mint leaves.

Sloe Gin Fizz

Alexander

Alexander

This creamy delight is more commonly made with brandy. The gin alternative shown here was especially popular in America in the '50s.

2 parts gin
1 part crème de cacao
1 part heavy cream
Cocoa powder, for dusting

Shake the ingredients vigorously in a cocktail shaker with cracked ice. Strain into a chilled cocktail glass and serve straight up. For the finishing touch, sprinkle with a fine dusting of cocoa powder.

Passionate Embrace

This seductive, thirst-quenching aphrodisiac is sure to get your blood racing! To vary the flavors, try different juices such as guava or mango. Remember to omit the sugar lump if using these, however, as they are sweeter and have a thicker texture than the passion fruit juice.

Sugar, for frosting
1 sugar lump, optional
1 tbsp brandy
1½ parts passion fruit
    juice, chilled
Sparkling dry white wine or
    champagne, chilled

Frost the rim of a chilled champagne flute with cold water and sugar (see p. 25). Set aside until ready to serve. Drop the sugar lump into the glass, if using. Pour in the brandy, then add the passion fruit juice. Top up with the sparkling wine or champagne and serve immediately.

2

Planet Cocktail

Out of this world

Thai Tiger

Thai Tiger

A crisp, clean cocktail combining the mixture of sweet and sour flavors that characterizes Thai food. It may look like lemonade but it's got a kick like a Thai boxer! Chili vodka may be used, but adding the fresh chili to plain vodka and shaking it well allows plenty of time for the heat and flavor to come through.

1 part lemon grass and
  ginger syrup (see recipe)
2 parts fresh coconut milk
1 part vodka
1 small chili, deseeded
  and sliced
1½ parts freshly squeezed
  lime juice
Sprite or 7-UP
Garnish
Stick of lemon grass
Sliver of chili
Slender wedge of lime

Combine the flavored syrup, coconut milk, vodka, sliced chili, and lime juice in a cocktail shaker with cracked ice. Shake well. Strain into a highball glass half-filled with crushed ice. Top up with Sprite or 7-UP. Garnish with a stick of lemon grass, a sliver of chili, and a slender wedge of lime.

Recipe

Sugar syrup can be made by measuring a ratio of two parts sugar to one part water into a saucepan. Stir over a gentle heat, then bring to the boil for 3–5 minutes. The longer you boil the sugar syrup, the more concentrated it will become. Cool, then pour into a bottle and refrigerate.

Make lemon grass and ginger syrup by adding 1 stick of crushed lemon grass, a 1in piece of peeled fresh ginger root cut into slivers, and one or two lime leaves to the pan while making ½ pint of sugar syrup.

Red October

A powerful blend of the proletarian and the bourgeois, the Red October is for wannabe revolutionaries and Muscovites everywhere. Garnish with a maraschino cherry or two for some pure Red Army chic!

1 part vodka
2 parts cherry brandy
7-UP
Maraschino cherries,
 to garnish

Shake the vodka and cherry brandy in a cocktail shaker with cracked ice. Strain into an old-fashioned glass half-filled with ice cubes. Fill with a little 7-UP. Garnish with maraschino cherries.

White Russian

A Black Russian is straight vodka and coffee liqueur, which is sometimes served over ice in a highball glass and topped up with cola. This variation is for those who love cocktails with a smooth, velvety texture.

2 parts vodka
1 part Kahlua or other
 coffee liqueur
1–1½ parts light cream

Shake the vodka and Kahlua or other coffee liqueur in a cocktail shaker with cracked ice. Strain into an ice-filled old-fashioned glass. Float cream on top using the back of a bar spoon.

Red October

Manhattan

Manhattan

This classic New York cocktail has spawned a host of variations over the years. Here is the original '50s version.

2 parts rye whisky
1 part dry vermouth
1 part sweet vermouth
Dash of Angostura bitters
Slice of lemon, to garnish

Stir the ingredients in a mixing glass with cracked ice. Strain into a cocktail glass and serve straight up. Garnish with a slice of lemon.

Scotch Fireball

This warming combination of classic Scotch and whisky liqueur has a mighty kick. Watch out—you might get burnt!

1 part Glayva
1 part Glenfiddich

Three-quarters fill a thin-stemmed glass with crushed ice and pour in the Glayva and Glenfiddich together. Stir gently.

Cuban Peach

You just can't beat the combination of brandy and rum for giving you that relaxing feeling. Lie back and enjoy!

1 part peach brandy
1 part white Cuban rum
1 tsp freshly squeezed
   lime juice
Pinch of sugar
Garnish
2 slices of peach
Sprig of fresh mint leaves

Combine the ingredients in a cocktail shaker with cracked ice. Shake well. Strain into a cocktail glass half-filled with crushed ice. Float two slices of peach and a sprig of mint on the top to garnish.

Frisco

"San Francisco! It is and has everything," said the poet Dylan Thomas in 1952—and that includes this exquisite cocktail, of course.

2 parts rye whisky
1 part Benedictine
½ part freshly squeezed
   lemon juice
Twist of lemon peel,
   to garnish

Shake the ingredients thoroughly in a cocktail shaker with cracked ice. Strain into a chilled cocktail glass and serve straight up. Garnish with a twist of lemon peel.

Cuban Peach

Polish Vodka Scoop

Polish Vodka Scoop

This cocktail may look like an ice cream, but the grassy flavor of the Zubrowka vodka is just enough of a giveaway. Use plain vodka if you want to deceive! You can reduce the sweetness by using club soda or tonic water instead of 7-UP.

2–3 small scoops lemon
  ice cream
1 part Zubrowka Bison
  Grass Vodka
7-UP
Twist of lemon peel,
  to garnish

Put the ice cream scoops into a chilled goblet or short-stemmed glass. Pour the vodka over the top, and top up with 7-UP. Garnish with a twist of lemon peel. Serve with a dessert spoon.

Bartender's Tip

To make a citrus "twist," take a piece of fresh fruit and cut a small oval piece of peel with no pith on it. Holding it above the cocktail glass, twist the peel between the thumb and forefinger of both hands. This action releases a delicate spray of citrus oil into the drink. Finally, drop the sliver of fruit into the drink.

Bronx

Johnnie Solon, the celebrated bartender at the old Waldorf-Astoria in Manhattan, christened this cocktail in honor of the Bronx Zoo.

2 parts gin
2 parts dry vermouth
1 part sweet vermouth
⅓ part orange juice
Twist of orange peel,
   to garnish

Shake the ingredients vigorously in a cocktail shaker with cracked ice. Strain into a chilled cocktail glass and serve straight up with a twist of orange peel.

Parisian Blonde

One of the greatest sex symbols in movie history, legendary French actress Brigitte Bardot was famous for her long, blonde, disheveled hair. Just like Bardot, this pale, smooth, and velvety cocktail has a certain "je ne sais quoi."

2 tbsp heavy cream
½ heaping tsp sugar
2 parts orange curaçao or
   Grand Marnier
1 part dark rum

Shake the ingredients vigorously in a cocktail shaker with cracked ice. Strain into a small chilled cocktail glass and serve straight up.

Bronx

Mexican Wave

Mexican Wave

Catch a slow roller or a tube wave, taste the salty sea breeze, and feel the warm
Mexican sun beating down on your shoulders . . . Close your eyes, take a sip, and
let this cocktail transport you to a tropical surfer's paradise.

1 part tequila
½ part crème de cassis
½ part sugar syrup (see p. 33)
Ginger ale
Slices of lime, to garnish

Shake the tequila, crème de cassis, and sugar
syrup in a cocktail shaker with cracked ice. Strain
into an old-fashioned glass, top up with ginger ale,
and mix with a glass swizzle stick. Float a few thin
lime slices on top to garnish.

Tijuana Café

This deliciously creamy coffee cocktail is the perfect way to end an evening meal.

5fl oz hot black coffee
1 part Kahlua or other
   coffee liqueur
1 tsp sugar
3 parts heavy cream,
   lightly whipped
1 cinnamon stick
Ground cinnamon,
   for dusting

Pour the hot coffee into a warmed heatproof
coffee glass. Stir in the liqueur and sugar, then
spoon the lightly whipped cream on top so that it
floats. Give it a gentle stir with a cinnamon stick
and dust with a little ground cinnamon.

Moscow Mule

Relations between the United States and the Soviet Union were strained in the '50s, as the name of this cocktail suggests! Kitschy mule accessories lend a touch of fun to this fantastic drink.

1½ parts vodka
1 tsp freshly squeezed
  lime juice
Ginger ale
Slice of lime, to garnish

Pour the vodka and the lime juice into a chilled highball glass one-third filled with ice cubes. Fill the glass to the brim with ginger ale. Garnish with a slice of lime.

Spanish Serenade

A tangy cocktail that instantly evokes the intoxicating enchantment of holiday romance, moonlit walks along the beach, and the passionate rhythm of the flamenco dancer. This summer sizzler is rich in aroma and decadent sweetness.

2 parts dry sherry
1½ parts Grand Marnier
Juice of ½ lemon
Juice of 1 orange
Twists of orange and lemon
  peel, to garnish

Mix the sherry and Grand Marnier with the lemon and orange juices in a mixing glass. Pour into a tall, ice-filled glass and garnish with twists of orange and lemon peel.

Moscow Mule

English Rose

English Rose

Parfait d'amour ("perfect love") is a violet liqueur whose subtle aromas and flavors are obtained from curaçao, orange peel, vanilla pods, almonds, and rose petals. The cool, refreshing color and flavor of the English Rose, with its classic '20s style, inspire elegance and sophistication.

3 parts extra dry vermouth
1½ parts kirsch
1 part Parfait d'amour

Combine the ingredients in a mixing glass with cracked ice. Stir well. Strain into a cocktail glass. Decorate by floating a rose petal or two on top.

Not Tonight Josephine

This potent combination would even render Napoleon harmless!

3 parts red wine
1 part Napoleon brandy
Dash of Pernod
Garnish
Cocktail onions
Maraschino cherry

Pour the red wine into a brandy glass with a couple of ice cubes. Add the brandy and Pernod. Stir, and garnish with cocktail onions and a maraschino cherry.

Limoncello Italiano

A beautiful "adult" version of lemonade.

2 parts vodka or citron
  vodka (see recipe)
½ part freshly squeezed
  lemon juice
½ part sugar syrup (see p. 33)
7-UP
Twist of lemon peel,
  to garnish

Shake the vodka, lemon juice, and sugar syrup
vigorously in a cocktail shaker with cracked ice.
Strain into a highball glass half-filled with crushed
ice and a long twist of lemon peel. Fill with 7-UP.

> **Recipe**
>
> Make citron vodka by steeping the pared rind from
> 6 lemons with 4oz/125g sugar in 24fl oz/750ml
> vodka, in a large jar. Shake the jar daily for
> 3–4 weeks. Once flavoring is complete, strain the
> vodka back into the vodka bottle. Serve chilled.

Miami

**In the '50s, New Yorkers often wintered in Florida, traveling there in luxurious
Pullman trains. This cocktail was a must for the in-car bartender's repertoire.**

5 parts light rum
2 parts freshly squeezed
  lemon juice
2 parts white crème
  de menthe
Twist of orange peel,
  to garnish

Shake the ingredients thoroughly in a cocktail
shaker with cracked ice. Strain into a chilled
cocktail glass and serve straight up. Garnish with
a twist of orange peel.

Limoncello Italiano

Havana Beach

Havana Beach

Sweet and light, this is one of the easiest rum cocktails to make on a summer's day. For ultimate refreshment, chop half a lime into four wedges and add to the cocktail shaker to give the drink a slightly sour lime flavor.

2 parts golden or white
  Cuban rum
3 parts pineapple juice
1 tsp sugar syrup (see p. 33)
Ginger ale
Pineapple cubes, to garnish

Shake the rum, pineapple juice, and sugar syrup vigorously in a cocktail shaker with cracked ice. Strain into an old-fashioned glass half-filled with ice cubes. Top up with ginger ale. Garnish with a few pineapple cubes.

Havana Cocktail

Dark and mysterious, this is a heady mixture, so sip it slowly.

1 part cream sherry
1 part golden rum
1 tsp freshly squeezed
  lemon or lime juice
Twist of lemon or lime peel,
  to garnish

Shake the ingredients thoroughly in a cocktail shaker with cracked ice. Strain into a cocktail glass. Garnish with a lemon or lime peel twist.

3

The New Romantics

Sexy cocktails for after dark

Glitterati

Glitterati

Opulent and luxurious, this variation on the classic Martini has the Midas touch!

2 parts vodka
Dash of dry vermouth
A shred of edible gold leaf
Garnish
Cocktail onion
Two olives

Combine the vodka, vermouth, and gold leaf in a mixing glass. Swirl with some very finely crushed ice to break up the gold leaf. Pour into a cocktail glass and serve straight up. Garnish with a cocktail onion and two black olives.

> **Bartender's Tip**
>
> Edible gold leaf is available from good delicatessens and specialist food and drink stores.

All Shook Up

Put on your blue suede shoes, dust off your cocktail shaker, and indulge in some rock 'n' roll with this zingy, fruity little number.

1oz frozen raspberries,
  thawed
1 part Martini Bianco
1½ parts gin
Frozen raspberries,
  to garnish

Rub the thawed raspberries through a sieve to remove the seeds, then shake the puree vigorously a cocktail shaker with the Martini, gin, and cracked ice. Pour into a cocktail glass and garnish with frozen raspberries.

Pink Lady

The addition of grenadine makes this drink a pretty Barbie-doll pink. Don't be fooled by appearances, though—it's more potent than it looks!

Grenadine syrup and sugar,
  for frosting
2 parts applejack
2 parts gin
1 part freshly squeezed
  lime juice
1 part grenadine
1 egg white
Maraschino cherry,
  to garnish

Frost the rim of a chilled cocktail glass with grenadine syrup and sugar (see p. 25). Shake the remaining ingredients in a cocktail shaker with cracked ice. Strain into the cocktail glass and serve straight up. Garnish with a maraschino cherry.

Moulin Rouge

Full of fun, fruitiness, and fizz—a few of these and you'll start singing and doing the high kicks without a stage!

4 parts pineapple juice
½ part brandy
Champagne or
  sparkling wine

Shake the pineapple juice and brandy thoroughly in a cocktail shaker with cracked ice. Strain into a highball glass half-filled with crushed ice. Top up with champagne or sparkling wine and stir.

Pink Lady

White Lady

White Lady

This shimmering, pure white cocktail is full of vintage Hollywood glamor. Imagine Marilyn Monroe sipping one of these wearing *that* white dress.

2 parts gin
1 part Cointreau or
   triple sec
1 part freshly squeezed
   lemon juice

Shake the ingredients thoroughly in a cocktail shaker with cracked ice. Strain into a chilled cocktail glass and serve straight up.

Silk Stockings

Why not slip into something a little more comfortable? Fusing a subtle blend of tempting chocolate and smooth cream with a suggestive splash of grenadine, this flirtatious little cocktail will be savored by amorous couples everywhere!

1 part tequila
½ part crème de cacao
½ tsp grenadine
2 tbsp heavy cream
Ground cinnamon,
   for dusting

Blend the tequila, crème de cacao, grenadine, and cream in a food processor with cracked ice to make an icy slush. Pour into a cocktail glass and dust with a little ground cinnamon to serve.

Bartender's Tip

If you don't have crème de cacao, try the coconut liqueur Malibu instead.

Millionaire

Sophistication in a glass—take a sip, close your eyes, and make a wish . . .

3 parts bourbon
1 part curaçao
1 egg white
½ part grenadine
Slice of orange, to garnish

Stir the ingredients well in a mixing glass with cracked ice. Strain into a chilled cocktail glass and serve straight up. Garnish with a slice of orange.

Between the Sheets

This cocktail was created in Harry's New York Bar in Paris in the '30s as a variation on the classic Sidecar. The addition of rum makes it a little more exciting, though still beautifully well balanced and refreshing.

1 part light rum
1 part brandy
1 part Cointreau or triple sec
1 part freshly squeezed
  lemon juice
½ part sugar syrup
  (optional—see p. 33)

Combine the rum, brandy, Cointreau or triple sec, lemon juice, and sugar syrup (if using) in a cocktail shaker with cracked ice. Shake well. Strain into a chilled cocktail glass and serve straight up.

Lemon Meringue Martini

Lemon Meringue Martini

This delicious cocktail tastes even better than lemon meringue pie! Smooth and creamy with a sharp lemon twang—and none of that soggy pastry!

2 parts citron vodka
1 part Drambuie
1 part freshly squeezed
   lemon juice
1–2 tsp sugar syrup
   (see p. 33)
Twist of lemon peel,
   to garnish

Shake all the ingredients thoroughly in a cocktail shaker with cracked ice. Strain into a cocktail or Margarita glass. Garnish with a lemon peel twist.

Double Vision

A great-tasting, refreshing vodka cocktail.

1 part citron vodka
1 part black currant vodka
1 part apple juice
1 part freshly squeezed
   lime juice
½ part sugar syrup (see p. 33)
3 dashes of Angostura bitters
Slice of apple, to garnish

Combine all the ingredients in a cocktail shaker with cracked ice. Shake well, and strain into a cocktail glass. Serve straight up garnished with a thin slice of apple.

Cosmopolitan

Also known as the "Stealth Martini," this sophisticated pink cocktail has a hidden kick! Popularized during the '80s as a yuppie status symbol, and more recently by *Sex and the City's* Carrie Bradshaw, this is a particular favorite with the affluent, young city dweller.

1½ parts citron vodka
1 part Cointreau or triple sec
1 part cranberry juice
Dash of orange bitters
Dash of freshly squeezed
  lime juice
Pared orange peel,
  to garnish

Shake all the ingredients thoroughly in a cocktail shaker with cracked ice. Strain into a chilled cocktail glass. Garnish with a piece of pared orange peel and serve straight up.

Red Sky at Night

Lie back on the porch with this wholesome cocktail, put your feet up, and admire the warmth of the setting sun and the firey hue of the evening sky.

Dash of freshly squeezed
  lemon juice
7-UP
½ part crème de cassis

Fill a chilled highball glass with ice and add a good dash of lemon juice. Pour in 7-UP to almost fill the glass, and stir in the crème de cassis.

Cosmopolitan

Blue Angel

Blue Angel

A heavenly drink with delicate floral and violet undertones, this attractive cocktail is beautiful when served with a slice of carambola.

1 part blue curaçao
1 part Parfait d'amour
1 part brandy
1 part freshly squeezed
   lemon juice
1 part light cream
Slice of carambola,
   to garnish

Shake all the ingredients in a cocktail shaker with cracked ice. Strain into a margarita glass. Garnish with a slice of carambola.

Kir

This cocktail was created by French farm laborers in Burgundy, who added crème de cassis to their Bourgogne Aligote wine to make it more palatable, and named the result after the colorful war hero and Mayor of Dijon, Canon Felix Kir. The usual ratio is 7 parts white wine to 1 part crème de cassis for a clean, crisp black currant flavor. If you're having a party, substitute champagne for white wine to create a Kir Royale.

½ part crème de cassis
Chilled dry white wine

Pour the crème de cassis into a large chilled wine glass or goblet, then top up with white wine and stir gently. Serve straight up.

Raspberry Crush

Here's a really quick way of making raspberry gin.

15 fresh raspberries
1 part gin
1 part framboise or
   sugar syrup (see p. 33)
Dash of freshly squeezed
   lemon juice
Club soda
Garnish
Frozen raspberries
Fresh mint leaves

Combine the fruit, gin, framboise or sugar syrup, and lemon juice with half a glass of crushed ice in a blender. Blend until pureed. Pour into an old-fashioned glass and add a little club soda to top up the glass. Garnish with frozen raspberries and fresh mint leaves.

Passionate Peach Fizz

Really fruity and a touch more exciting than that old favorite the Buck's Fizz.

2 parts orange juice
2 parts passion fruit juice
½ part peach schnapps
Champagne or sparkling wine
Wedge of peach, to garnish

Shake the fruit juices and peach schnapps vigorously in a cocktail shaker with cracked ice. Strain into a champagne flute and top up with champagne or sparkling wine. Serve straight up with a wedge of peach.

Raspberry Crush

Saketini

Saketini

Though often referred to as "rice wine," sake is, in fact, a rice beer. It is traditionally served warm in small cups in Japanese restaurants, but can also be served at room temperature, or even chilled. The subtle, orangey notes of the sake make the Saketini a mouthwatering appetizer cocktail.

2 parts sake
1 part vodka
½ part gin
½ part Cointreau or
  triple sec
Garnish
Slice of cucumber
Sliver of scallion

Combine the ingredients with cracked ice in a mixing glass. Stir and strain into a cocktail glass. Serve straight up and garnish with a slice of cucumber and sliver of scallion.

Coq Rouge

This old favorite seems to have fallen out of fashion recently. Time for a revival!

2 parts light rum
1 part gin
1 part freshly squeezed
  lemon or lime juice
1 part Cointreau or triple sec
Twist of orange peel,
  to garnish

Stir or shake the ingredients with cracked ice. Strain into a chilled cocktail glass and serve straight up. Garnish with a twist of orange peel.

Ab Fab

In homage to Patsy and Edina from *Absolutely Fabulous*, this cocktail was created in London, using their favorites—"Bolly" and "Stoli."

1 part Stolichnaya vodka
2 parts cranberry and
  raspberry juice
Bollinger champagne

Shake the vodka and cranberry and raspberry juice in a cocktail shaker with cracked. Strain into a cocktail glass and top up with champagne. Serve straight up.

Romantic Blue Lagoon

Immerse yourself in this refreshing and thirst-quenching aquamarine cocktail.

1 part blue curaçao
1 part vodka
Dash freshly squeezed
  lemon juice
10fl oz lemonade
Slices of carambola,
  to garnish

Pour the curaçao and vodka into a cocktail glass filled with crushed ice. Add the lemon juice, mix with a glass swizzle stick, and top up with the lemonade. Garnish with slices of carambola.

Bartender's Tip

If you don't have blue curaçao, use another orange-flavored liqueur such as Grand Marnier, Cointreau, or triple sec, and add a dash of blue food coloring for the desired effect.

Ab Fab

4

Club Tropicana

Tropical teasers

Piña Colada

Translating from the Spanish as "strained pineapple," the Piña Colada started life in the Caribbean and combines many of the island's natural wonders: pineapple, coconut, and, of course, rum. The all-time favorite summer beach cocktail, this is a gorgeous, creamy fruit creation.

2 parts golden, white, or dark rum
3 parts pineapple juice or ½ cup diced pineapple pieces
1 part coconut cream or fresh coconut milk
½ part light cream
2 dashes of Angostura bitters (optional)
Garnish
Wedge of pineapple
Maraschino cherry

Combine all ingredients with four or five ice cubes in a blender. Blend until smooth. Pour into a large goblet or Boston glass. Garnish with a wedge of pineapple and a maraschino cherry.

Piña Colada

Mai Tai

Mai Tai

The Mai Tai was created by Victor "Trader Vic" Bergeron, who was famous for his rum-based cocktails. He made it in his San Francisco bar one night in 1944, then asked two friends from Tahiti to try it. "Mai tai . . . roa ae!" said one of them, which translates as "Out of this world . . . the best!"

1 part light rum
½ part dark rum
1 part orange juice
1 part apricot brandy
½ part tequila
½ part Cointreau or
  triple sec
2 dashes of grenadine
Dash of Amaretto or orgeat
Dash of Angostura bitters
Garnish
Slices of orange, lemon,
  and lime
Maraschino cherry
Sprig of fresh mint

Shake the ingredients vigorously in a cocktail shaker with cracked ice. Strain into an old-fashioned glass or large goblet half-filled with crushed ice. Garnish with slices of orange, lemon, and lime, a maraschino cherry, and a sprig of mint.

Buena Vista

"Buena vista" means a good view—the perfect description of this dazzlingly transparent aqua-blue cocktail that is beautiful to sip while you daydream.

1 part white rum
1 part blue curaçao
1 part sugar syrup (see p. 33)
1 part freshly squeezed
  lime juice
Wedge of lemon, to garnish

Shake the ingredients vigorously in a cocktail shaker with cracked ice. Strain into a highball glass. Garnish with a wedge of lemon.

Acapulco Gold

A daiquiri by any other name, this is a smooth, tropical cocktail that's so delicious, you could drink it all day!

2 parts pineapple juice
1 part grapefruit juice
1 part tequila
1 part golden rum
1 part coconut milk

Combine all the ingredients in a cocktail shaker with cracked ice. Shake well. Strain into a Boston glass half-filled with ice cubes. Decorate with a fun straw and a monkey in a palm tree.

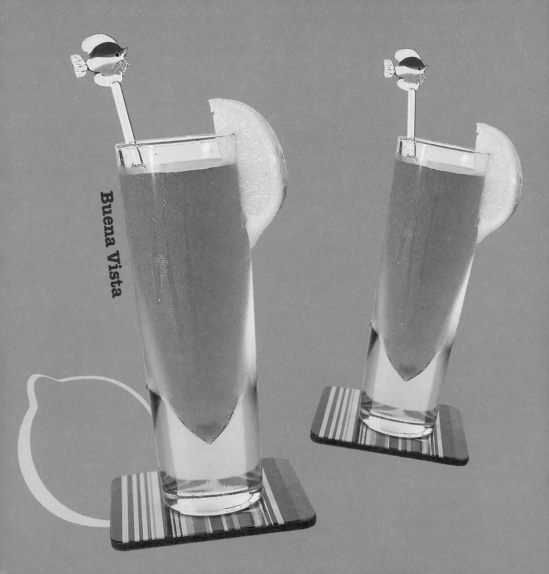

Buena Vista

Tequila Sunrise

Tequila Sunrise

The Tequila Sunrise may have originated at the Agua Caliente racetrack in Mexico in Prohibition times, when Californians crossed the border to take part in the races and enjoy legal hits of liquor. After a long night of imbibing, a pick-me-up of tequila and nutritious orange juice would have seemed just the thing!

2 parts tequila
5 parts orange juice
½ part grenadine
Garnish
Slice of orange
Maraschino cherry

Pour the tequila and orange juice into a highball glass filled with ice. Stir. When it settles, pour the grenadine in a circle around the top of the drink and let it fall to the bottom. Garnish with a slice of orange and a maraschino cherry.

Almond Breeze

Considered a ladies' drink back in the '50s, this refreshing mixture of pure orange juice and gin can now be enjoyed by everyone.

1 part gin
1 part orange juice
Slice of orange, to garnish

Shake the ingredients vigorously in a cocktail shaker with cracked ice. Strain into a chilled old-fashioned glass and serve straight up. Garnish with a slice of orange.

Daiquiri

An American classic, the daiquiri originates from the iron mines in the Cuban town of Daiquiri around the turn of the century, when American mining engineers drank a mixture of the local rum, lime juice, and sugar to ward off tropical fevers. Nowadays, you don't need any excuse to enjoy it!

3 parts light rum
1 part freshly squeezed
   lime juice
½ tsp sugar syrup (see p. 33)
Garnish
Slice of lime
Maraschino cherry

Shake the ingredients in a cocktail shaker with cracked ice. Strain into a chilled hurricane or highball glass and serve straight up. Garnish with a slice of lime and a maraschino cherry.

Knickerbocker

Use the syrups from canned raspberries and pineapple to give this glorious drink a refreshing and tangy sweetness.

5 parts light rum
1 part freshly squeezed
   lemon juice
1 part raspberry syrup
1 part pineapple syrup
Garnish
Twists of orange peel
Maraschino cherry

Shake the ingredients thoroughly in a cocktail shaker with cracked ice. Strain into a chilled cocktail glass and serve straight up. Garnish with twists of orange peel and a maraschino cherry.

Daiquiri

Sparkling Bouquet

Sparkling Bouquet

This spectacular melon-flavored cocktail has an aura of psychedelic '60s flower power but with a touch more subtlety in both looks, and fruity, flowery tones. For added fragrance, add a dash of elderflower syrup to the sparkling wine.

1 part melon liqueur
Sparkling wine, chilled

Pour the melon liqueur into a cocktail glass or champagne saucer. Top up with the sparkling wine and decorate with fragrant petals and flowers.

Zombie

A zombie is a snake god of voodoo cults in West Africa, Haiti, and the Southern US. According to voodoo belief, it can use its supernatural powers to enter into and reanimate a corpse. This refreshing drink will give you a new lease of life!

1 part dark rum
1 part light rum
1 part golden rum
½ part apricot brandy
½ part curaçao
2 parts orange juice
2 parts pineapple juice
½ part grenadine syrup
1 part freshly squeezed
   lime juice
Twist of orange peel,
   to garnish

Shake the ingredients vigorously in a cocktail shaker with cracked ice. Strain into an ice-filled Boston glass. Float ½ part overproof rum (see tip) on top. Garnish with a long twist of orange peel.

Bartender's Tip

Overproof or high-strength rum is any rum with over 57% alcohol per volume.

Harvey Wallbanger

This is a classic Screwdriver, spiked with Galliano, as preferred by Harvey, a Californian surfer in the '70s. Legend has it that, on leaving his local bar one night after several of these, he walked into the wall with his surfboard. He was nicknamed "The Wallbanger," and the rest is history!

4 parts orange juice
2 parts vodka
½ part Galliano
Orange slices, to garnish

Pour the orange juice and the vodka into a highball glass filled with ice cubes. Stir, and then carefully add the Galliano to float on the top. Garnish with orange slices.

Windward Island

Dark, cool, and refreshing, this tropical cocktail is perfect for those people who enjoy their cola with an added depth.

1 part golden rum
½ part Tia Maria
Cola
Orange slices, to garnish

Shake the rum and Tia Maria vigorously in a cocktail shaker with cracked ice. Strain into an old-fashioned glass almost filled with ice cubes. Top up with cola, and garnish with orange slices.

Harvey Wallbanger

Singapore Sling

Singapore Sling

The Singapore Sling was created by the barman at Singapore's Raffles Hotel in 1915. Today, any visit to Singapore is incomplete without sampling one of these world-famous cocktails.

2 parts gin
1 part cherry brandy
½ part freshly squeezed
  lemon juice
Dash of Benedictine
Dash of Cointreau or
  triple sec
Club soda
Garnish
Orange and lemon slices
Maraschino cherry

Shake the gin, cherry brandy, lemon juice, Benedictine, and Cointreau in a cocktail shaker with cracked ice. Strain into a chilled Collins glass. Add ice cubes and club soda to fill the glass. Garnish with orange and lemon slices and a maraschino cherry.

Almond Breeze

This cocktail looks like an innocent bubbly lime lemonade—but watch out—it has hidden depths!

1 part white rum
½ part Dash of Amaretto
  or orgeat
½ part melon liqueur
Tonic water

Shake the rum, dash of Amaretto or orgeat, and melon liqueur in a cocktail shaker with cracked ice. Strain into a highball glass, half-filled with crushed ice. Top up with tonic water.

Caribbean Champagne Cocktail

This zingy cocktail looks and tastes delightfully decadent!

¼ part light rum
¼ part crème de banane
Dash of Angostura bitters
Chilled champagne
Garnish
Slices of banana
Maraschino cherry
Pineapple leaf

Pour the rum, crème de banane, and Angostura bitters into a champagne flute. Top with champagne and stir gently with a glass swizzle stick. Garnish with slices of banana, a maraschino cherry, and a pineapple leaf.

Kiwi Kraze

This terrific cocktail is especially tasty when made with fresh kiwi fruit, although using the ready-made juice is less time-consuming.

3 parts kiwi fruit juice
1 part gin
Dash of absinthe
Tonic water
Slice of kiwi fruit, to garnish

Shake the kiwi juice, gin, and a good dash of absinthe in a cocktail shaker with cracked ice. Strain into an old-fashioned glass half-filled with crushed ice. Top up with tonic water. Garnish with a slice of kiwi fruit.

Caribbean Champagne Cocktail

Sea Mist

Sea Mist

A close relative of the Sea Breeze, one of the cocktails that became popular in New York in the mid-'90s, this variation blends cranberry and raspberry juice with pink grapefruit juice for the ultimate fresh-fruit sensation.

3 parts cranberry and
  raspberry juice
3 parts pink grapefruit juice
2 parts vodka
Slices of lime and lemon
  frozen in ice cubes

Shake the fruit juices and vodka thoroughly in a cocktail shaker with cracked ice. Strain into a highball glass filled with decorated ice cubes.

Tropical Temptation

This potent tropical smoothie is a seductive and thirst-quenching aphrodisiac. Create the perfect tonic—pour pure nectar over crushed ice, flirt with the mingling flavors and feel the full-bodied tonic hit the spot!

4oz pineapple pieces
  in syrup
3½ parts coconut cream
5 parts chilled tropical
  fruit juice
Juice of ½ lime
2½ parts dark rum
Garnish
Maraschino cherries
Lime slices
Sprig of fresh mint

Set aside two pieces of pineapple. Blend the remaining ingredients in a food processor with four or five ice cubes until smooth. Pour into a large chilled goblet. Garnish with the reserved pineapple pieces, maraschino cherries, lime slices, and fresh mint.

5

Super Sharp Shooters

Hot shots for instant enlightenment

Bazooka Joe Shooter

Fabulous colors and fascinating to create, this shooter could be highly explosive!

½ part blue curaçao
½ part crème de banane
½ part Irish cream liqueur

Pour the curaçao into a shot glass, followed by the crème de banane. Float the Irish cream liqueur on top by pouring it carefully over the back of a teaspoon. The yellow crème de banane will sink to the bottom and mix with the curaçao to create a luminous green layer beneath the Irish cream.

Angel's Kiss

This truly heavenly tasting shooter has a smooth velvety surface and rich coffee undertones. Dust with cocoa powder before serving for the finishing touch.

1½ parts Tia Maria, chilled
2 tbsp heavy cream
Unsweetened cocoa powder,
  for dusting

Pour the Tia Maria into a shot glass. Float the cream on top by pouring it carefully into the glass over the back of a teaspoon so that it floats on the surface of the Tia Maria, forming a separate layer. Dust the cream with the cocoa powder, and serve.

Bazooka Joe Shooter

Sol y Sombre

Sol y Sombre

The colorless, licorice-flavored liqueur anisette combines with brandy in this layered shooter, mixing light with dark, sun with shade. Watch out—like the sun, the brandy burns as it goes down!

1 part anisette
1 part brandy

Pour the anisette into a shot glass and carefully add the brandy over the back of a bar spoon so that it sits on top of the anisette.

B52

This classic multilayered combination of Kahlua, Baileys, and Grand Marnier makes for a smooth and subtle shooter. Knock it down in one, just how the Russian KGB drink theirs!

½ part Kahlua or other coffee liqueur
½ part Baileys or other Irish cream liqueur
½ part Grand Marnier

Pouring delicately over a bar spoon, add the coffee liqueur, the Irish Cream, then the Grand Marnier liqueur to a shot glass in that order. Serve without mixing.

Tempting Trio

Three cream liqueur flavors in one glass—delicious!

½ part green crème
  de menthe
½ part crème de banane
½ part Baileys or other Irish
  cream liqueur

Carefully layer the crème de menthe, crème de banane, and Irish cream liqueur into a shot glass over the back of a bar spoon.

Little Devil

Whether you're a fallen angel, a little minx, or a handsome devil, you're sure to enjoy this tongue-teasing aperitif. For a dramatic serving suggestion, add indoor sparklers to the prepared cocktail before serving.

½ part freshly squeezed
  lemon juice
½ part Cointreau or
  triple sec
1 part dark rum
1 part gin

Shake all the ingredients vigorously in a cocktail shaker with cracked ice. Strain into a shot glass, and serve immediately.

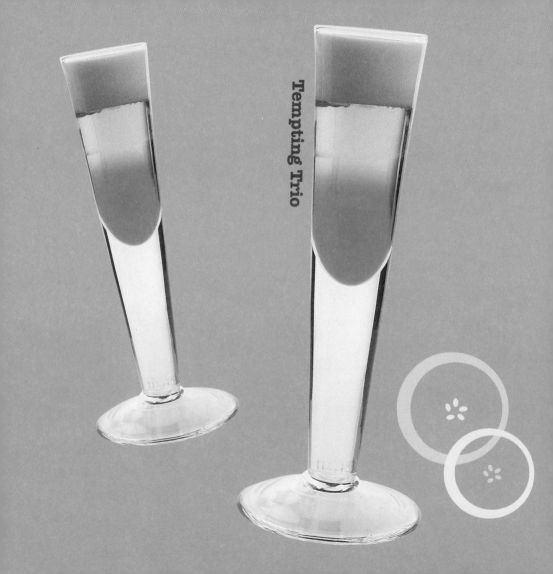

Tempting Trio

Dangerous Detox

Dangerous Detox

A detox shooter with an added layer of danger! Not easy to construct, but if you succeed, you deserve to sample this fantastic combination of flavors.

½ part peach schnapps
½ part cranberry juice
½ part vodka
Dash of absinthe

Carefully pour the ingredients over the back of a teaspoon into a shot glass in order of density, as listed, so that you have three equal layers and a thin green line of absinthe at the top.

Basil Vice

This dainty shooter is a delicious palate cleanser—great between courses, or to spur your taste-buds into action at the start of a meal.

2 basil leaves
½ part vodka
Dash of raspberry syrup

Roll the basil leaves up tightly, cut into thin strips and chop finely. Place in the bottom of a shot glass, then almost fill with crushed ice. Pour in the vodka, stir and add a dash of raspberry syrup.

Electric Flag

You'll need skill and practice to knock this one back all in one go!

½ part grenadine syrup
½ part Parfait d'amour
½ part kirsch or grappa

Pour the grenadine syrup into a shot glass. Carefully add the Parfait d'amour and then the kirsch or grappa, layering each ingredient over the back of a bar spoon.

Flaming Sambuca

This pyrotechnic cocktail need not be the preserve of chemistry geeks. There are a variety of different techniques, depending on your level of daring—and how keen you are on singed eyebrow chic!

2 parts sambuca
3 coffee beans

Pour the sambuca into a shot glass, add the coffee beans, and ignite. You should see a small blue flame. Extinguish the with your palm, inhale the fumes from the glass, then swallow in one.

Bartender's Tip

One word of warning: the longer you leave the glass flaming, the hotter it will get! Remember—always be careful with fire.

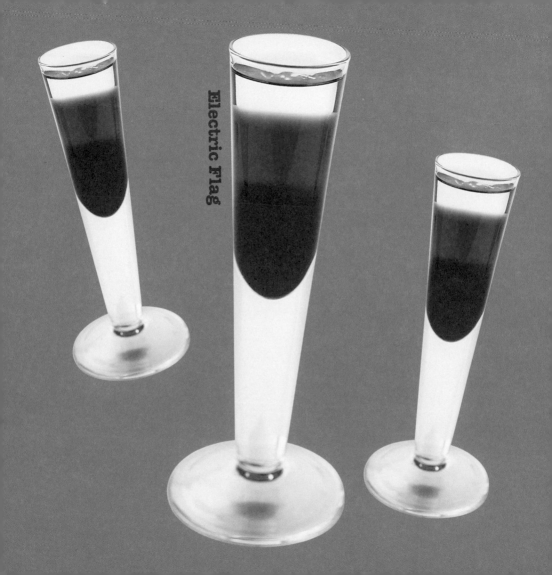

Electric Flag

Glass Shapes

Boston glass

Brandy snifter

Champagne flute

Shot glass

Champagne saucer

Cocktail glass

Old fashioned glass

Collins glass

Goblet

Highball glass

Wine glass

Hurricane glass

Irish coffee cream

Margarita glass

Index